The New World

1500–1750

SADDLEBACK
EDUCATIONAL PUBLISHING

Saddleback's *Graphic American History*

SADDLEBACK
EDUCATIONAL PUBLISHING
www.sdlback.com

ISBN-13: 978-1-59905-356-1
ISBN-10: 1-59905-356-X
eBook: 978-1-60291-684-5

Printed in Malaysia

20 19 18 17 16   7 8 9 10 11

DISCOVERING AMERICA!

Christopher Columbus set sail for Asia in 1492 but reached what are now known as the Caribbean islands instead. Thinking he had reached India, he called the islands he found the Indies, and the natives, Indians.

The first voyage lasted five weeks. To the fearful sailors on unknown seas, it seemed endless. Upon reaching land, Columbus stepped ashore carrying a holy banner and claimed the land for Spain, while the natives stared at their strange visitors.

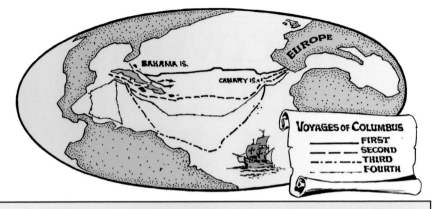

VOYAGES OF COLUMBUS
————— FIRST
— — — SECOND
—··—··— THIRD
—·—·—· FOURTH

On later voyages, Columbus explored the Bahamas, Cuba, the Virgin Islands, and Puerto Rico. He established the first permanent European settlement in the New World on the island of Santo Domingo, which he called *Hispaniola*. Not finding the riches he had hoped for, he divided the land and the Indians who lived on it among the Spanish settlers.

The natives who refused to work on the great sugar and cotton plantations were either killed or shipped to Spain to be sold as slaves.

Great numbers of slaves were then imported from Africa to work the plantations.

Within 50 years the 300,000 original natives of Hispaniola had been wiped out.

For 50 years after Columbus, Spain had no rivals in the New World. Spanish *conquistadores** first conquered the islands and then advanced to the mainland.

Juan Ponce de León, having conquered Puerto Rico, set sail again in search of a miraculous fountain of youth of which he had heard.

On Easter morning, he came upon a land which he named *Florida*, in honor of the day (*Pascua Florida*, or Flowering Easter).

Although he tramped through jungles and bathed in many springs, he sailed away again no younger than when he had arrived.

*Conquerors, soldiers, and explorers

4

In Haiti, Vasco Balboa hid in a barrel to smuggle himself aboard a ship sailing to Darien on the Isthmus of Panama. At Darien, he heard stories from the natives of gold and silver and a great sea beyond the mountains.

To find these treasures, he led a band of Spaniards through jungles across the isthmus.

After 20 days, he saw from a mountain peak the waters of the Pacific Ocean.

Reaching the sea after four more days, he walked into the water, claiming it and the lands it touched for the King of Spain. He called it the South Sea. He never dreamed that it was the world's largest ocean.

The Spaniards dreamed of finding gold and other treasure. In 1519, Fernando Cortes sailed from Cuba with 11 ships and more than 500 soldiers and invaded Mexico. He defeated the Aztec rulers and captured and killed their emperor, Montezuma. He took gold, silver, and jewels.

Ten years later, Francisco Pizarro invaded Peru, conquered the Inca rulers there, and found still greater treasure. The Spaniards took over the gold and silver mines of Mexico and Peru. To work the mines, they used native labor and many slaves imported from Africa.

Pack trains carried the wealth across the Andes Mountains to Panama.

From Panama, treasure fleets sailed twice a year for Spain.

This wealth led other explorers to travel thousands of miles in a search for more.

One such group of 300 men was shipwrecked in a hurricane on the Gulf of Texas. Only four men survived.

Later he escaped. On the Texas coast he came across three other survivors—two Spaniards and an African slave, Estavanico.

One of these was Cabeza de Vaca. He waded onto Galveston Island, where the Native Americans captured him and made him a slave.

These men traveled on foot from tribe to tribe of Native Americans for over 2,000 miles... through west Texas, up the Colorado River, across the Pecos and the Rio Grande. They were the first Europeans to visit New Mexico and Arizona.

Vaca became famous as a medicine man who cured the sick by using prayers and the sign of the cross.

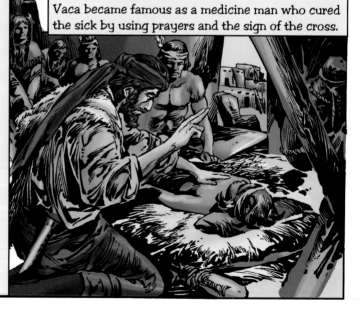

Estavanico carried a gourd rattle that the Native Americans believed was magic. He became an idol. Crowds gathered everywhere, believing their wounds would be healed and the sick cured by touching the garments of these castaways. They brought gifts to them such as beads, buffalo skins, and pearls.

For eight years the four men wandered among the Native Americans before at last reaching a Spanish settlement in Mexico. They then returned to Spain where Vaca published an account of their sufferings.

He told of squash and corn grown by the Native Americans, foods that were unknown to Europeans.

He told of the "hunchback cows" that covered the plains as far as the eye could see.

He also told of native stories of rich cities to the north, with walls of gold set with emeralds—the Seven Cities of Cibola. And this is what people remembered.

Hernando de Soto was a nobleman who had been with Pizarro in Peru. He wanted to discover treasure of his own. In 1539, after hearing Vaca's stories, he led the fanciest Spanish expedition of all into the Florida wilderness.

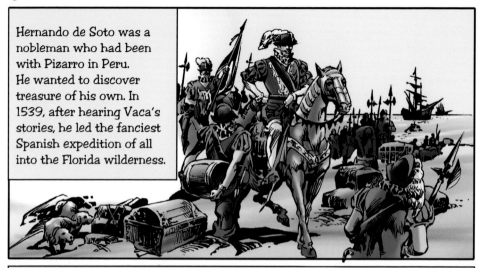

For months they marched through Georgia, Alabama, and Mississippi, finding only poor Native American villages. Their food and supplies gave out. They were ill, and at least 200 men died.

At last they stumbled upon the mile-wide Mississippi River.

They hollowed out logs to make canoes and crossed into Arkansas.

To the Native Americans, de Soto posed as a god, using his mirror to make magic.

De Soto died of fever. His men were afraid to let the Native Americans know that he was a mortal man. They disposed of his body in the Mississippi River, secretly, at night.

For de Soto there were no Seven Cities and no gold. But another Spanish group did find the Seven Cities.

In 1540, Francisco de Coronado led an expedition northward from Mexico into New Mexico and Arizona. He had heard Vaca's tales of the Zuni warriors, fierce fighters with an ancient civilization.

The Zunis built houses of baked earth and rock, four and five stories high, with as many as a thousand rooms together, and located on high cliffs. When the desert sun shone on these cliff cities, they sparkled as if made of gold.

The Zunis fought fiercely to protect their town. When the Spaniards finally captured it, they found they had conquered only a village of earth and rock.

There were Seven Cities of Cibola—seven little villages like this one, all worthless to the Spanish treasure seekers.

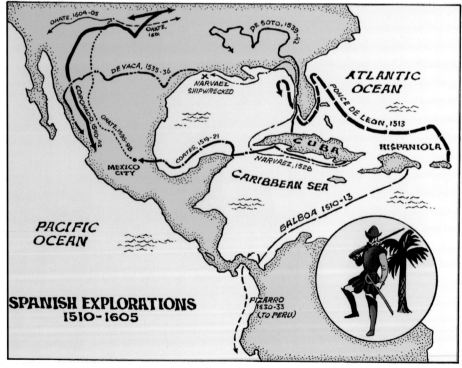

SPANISH EXPLORATIONS 1510-1605

For 50 years Spain had no rivals in America. But in the 1530s Jacques Cartier, a French seaman, made several voyages to Canada, claiming that country for the French.

Cartier sailed his ships far up the broad St. Lawrence River to the present site of Quebec. They received a warm welcome from friendly natives, who brought food and led them to an Indian town.

Here the sick and crippled approached, begging Cartier to cure them. He read from the Gospel and made the sign of the cross over them.

He also gave gifts, including small rings that the children scrambled for.

During a long, cold winter, the Frenchmen listened to native tales of a northern kingdom with mines of gold, silver, and rubies. But this kingdom could not be found, and they returned to France with no treasure.

In the summers following, French fishermen landed on the Canadian coast of Newfoundland. They found the natives there had furs to trade for axes, iron kettles, and cloth. Furs were highly valued in Europe.

The fishermen learned to bring a supply of trading goods. Fishing stations became trading posts. This began the French fur trade, which spread inland and led to the building of a chain of trading posts such as Port Royal, Quebec, and Montreal, which later became towns or cities.

Samuel de Champlain was a French naval officer who devoted himself to making Canada a French colony, to exploring it, and to making the fur trade profitable.

Under the "rock of Quebec," on the St. Lawrence, Champlain founded the settlement that would grow into a great Canadian city. The name, in Algonquin, meant "beware of the rock."

Champlain went on to explore the lake named for him as well as Lakes George, Ontario, and Huron. He became a warm friend of the Algonquin and Huron peoples and took to the warpath with them against their enemies, the Iroquois.

When Champlain fired his arquebus,* which held four bullets, two Iroquois were killed, a third wounded. The others ran away in fright. From that time, the Iroquois were bitter enemies of the French.

The French pushed westward along the inland waterways, the first real explorers of the interior of North America. Among the French explorers were many brave Jesuit priests who carried their Catholic religion to the natives of mid-America.

Father Louis Hennepin was the first white man to see and describe the wonders of Niagara Falls.

* Old-fashioned type of matchlock gun

Father Marquette and his friend Joliet, with a party of only seven men, paddled hundreds of miles to find the great Mississippi River.

One day, as they approached an Illinois Indian village, a man called a greeting to them.

How beautiful is the sun, O Frenchmen, when thou comest to visit us. All our town awaits thee.

Father Marquette gave the natives gifts and spoke of God as their Creator. Afterward the Frenchmen were entertained at a feast. They were served fish and wild ox as well as a boiled cornmeal dish, which was fed to them by the spoonful as to children.

They reached the Mississippi River and traveled toward its mouth. They visited many Native American tribes. They took a different route for their home-ward journey and reached Lake Michigan.

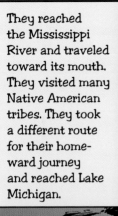

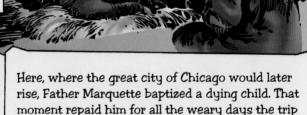

Here, where the great city of Chicago would later rise, Father Marquette baptized a dying child. That moment repaid him for all the weary days the trip had taken.

Thus, steady with a line of forts and trading posts, the French marked out an empire. Robert la Salle was perhaps the greatest of the French explorers. His biggest achievement was to sail through the heart of America from Canada through the Great Lakes and down the Mississippi River to the Gulf of Mexico.

In 1682, at the mouth of the Mississippi, La Salle planted a cross and claimed the Mississippi River valley for France, naming it Louisiana in honor of King Louis XIV.

One hundred years after Columbus, there was still no permanent English settlement in America. But in 1607, 104 Englishmen, sponsored by the London Company, reached the Virginia coast in three small ships. They sailed 30 miles up a river they named the James, and landed at a site they called Jamestown.

The first afternoon, as they returned to their boats after exploring the site, the Native Americans attacked.

They managed to make peace, but they quickly set to work building a fort.

The settlers had come believing they would find diamonds and rubies on the beaches of Virginia and gold everywhere. They had not expected to work.

After their ships sailed for England, everything went wrong. Men were starving. Swamp mosquitoes spread disease, and many died. At the end of five months, not five men were capable of standing guard at the fort.

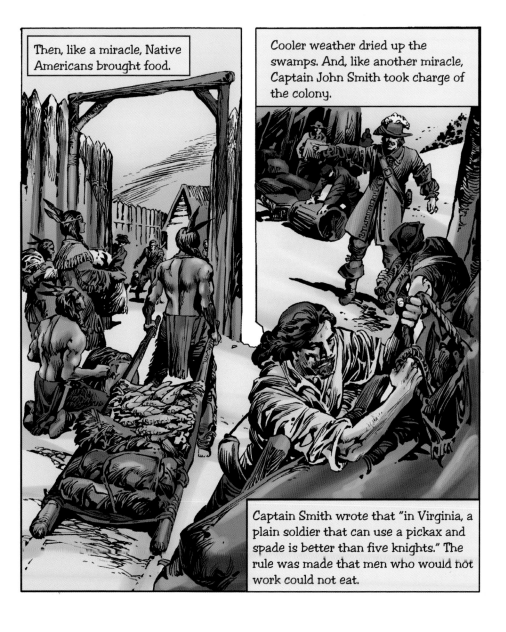

Then, like a miracle, Native Americans brought food.

Cooler weather dried up the swamps. And, like another miracle, Captain John Smith took charge of the colony.

Captain Smith wrote that "in Virginia, a plain soldier that can use a pickax and spade is better than five knights." The rule was made that men who would not work could not eat.

On the voyage from England, Smith had been accused of conspiring to become king. He was imprisoned, tried, and let go. Now his strict control saved the colony.

When soft-handed men swore at their blisters, Smith ordered a can of cold water poured down the swearer's sleeve, one can for each oath.

Before winter, 20 houses and a church were completed. Smith also bartered successfully with the Native Americans for food to see the colonists through the winter.

Then more settlers arrived. Captain Smith returned to England, and the colony fell apart again. There were more starving times. Soon another remarkable man arrived and helped the colony to its final success.

In 1614, John Rolfe, an English gentleman, and Pocahontas, an Algonquin princess, were married in the church at Jamestown.

Pocahontas was the daughter of Powhatan, the powerful chief of the Algonquin Indians. This marriage, and Rolfe's understanding of the Indians, led to peace between Indians and settlers for several years.

Rolfe made history a second way. He planted seeds of a type of tobacco grown in the Caribbean Islands. It flourished in Virginia.

It was sweeter and milder than the native tobacco. The demand for it in Europe was so great that even the streets of Jamestown were planted with it.

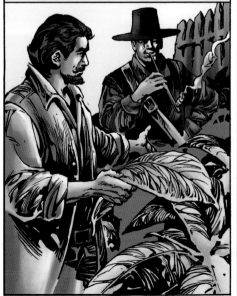

At last the colonists had a money crop. They were soon given ways to spend it.

In 1619, ships arrived carrying "young maidens," to be given as wives to those settlers who would pay 120 pounds of tobacco for their transportation.

A Dutch ship arrived with a different cargo—20 African slaves for sale.

Raising tobacco required labor. The slaves proved invaluable in the tobacco fields.

Also that year, the governor called together a legislative assembly.

With two representatives from each of the little settlements around Jamestown, this body met to pass the laws by which they would be governed—the first such body in America.

In England, King James I claimed the right to tell his subjects how to worship. A group of religious people differed with the king and wanted to set up a separate church.

At last these separatists decided to brave the dangers of the New World, America, to set up their own state where they could worship in their own way. The Pilgrims, as they became known in history, left Plymouth, England, on the tiny ship *Mayflower*, on September 6, 1620.

About 100 in number, they sailed with tears and prayers.

For weeks, fierce Atlantic storms tossed the ship like a cork.

They patched leaks everywhere and propped a sagging main beam.

Land ho!

After a weary 65 days, they sighted the Massachusetts coast.

Before going ashore on November 11, they drew up an agreement, which every male passenger signed, promising to pass and obey such laws as should be for the general good. This Mayflower Compact was one of the seeds from which our democracy grew.

The spot where they landed was named Plymouth, after the English port. During the first hard winter, half of them died from cold or disease. But spring came, and they worked on with courage and determination.

One day Chief Massasoit arrived with 60 warriors. They could have wiped out the weakened Pilgrims.

But the Wampanoag Indians offered friendship and help.

They taught the settlers to grow corn ...

... to trap and skin beavers ...

... to fish and to catch game.

That fall, when the corn crop was gathered, they held a harvest festival.

On this first Thanksgiving with the Native Americans, the settlers feasted, played games, and gave thanks to God.

The Pilgrims, who settled Plymouth Plantation in Massachusetts, founded a democracy. Puritan settlers arrived later, 1630, with a charter that established the Massachusetts Bay Colony. By 1634, some 10,000 Puritans had arrived. Boston and Salem were among the many towns founded in that area.

Puritan settlers put together a church-state in which everyone lived and worshipped God according to strict Puritan rules. The church was supported by taxes, but any man, rich or poor, could vote if he was a good church member.

The meeting house was both church and town hall. The ministers and elders of the church kept strict watch over the rulers.

For failing to attend church, someone might be put in the stocks.

For whispering in church, he or she might be ducked in the public pond.

Roger Williams was a young minister who protested against the rule of the church. He was ordered to leave Massachusetts forever.

Instead of returning to England, he followed a Native American path through the snow to Narragansett Bay.

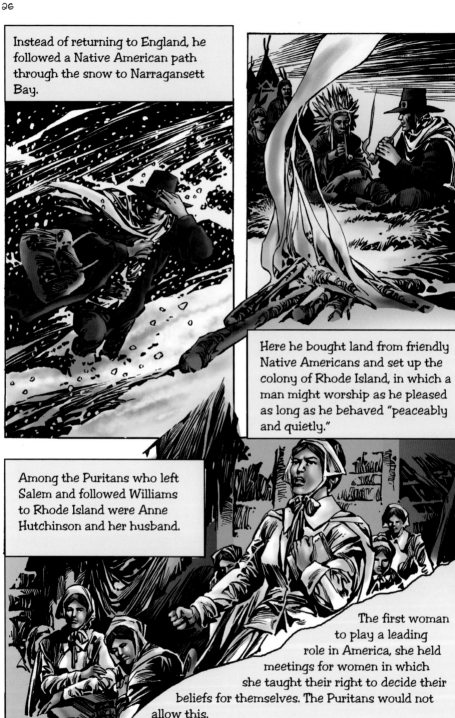

Here he bought land from friendly Native Americans and set up the colony of Rhode Island, in which a man might worship as he pleased as long as he behaved "peaceably and quietly."

Among the Puritans who left Salem and followed Williams to Rhode Island were Anne Hutchinson and her husband.

The first woman to play a leading role in America, she held meetings for women in which she taught their right to decide their beliefs for themselves. The Puritans would not allow this.

The New England Puritans took education as seriously as they took their religious doctrines. As early as 1647, Massachusetts law required every town of 50 families to support an elementary school.

Every town of 100 families had to have a grammar school in which boys could be prepared for college. The idea of general education was one of New England's greatest contributions to the country.

Harvard College was founded by a grant from the Bay State Assembly in 1630. The new town of Cambridge donated a building, and in 1638 the college opened in a small house in a cow-yard owned by the town.

Perhaps this proved convenient in the 1640s, when many students paid their college bills with farm produce and cattle. From the first, however, the college set a high standard of scholarship, attracting students from as far away as Bermuda and England itself.

28

Though setting a fine example in education, Massachusetts, in 1692, set a bad example in mass hysteria. Most people in the Western world, including ministers and men of science, believed that a person could make a bargain with the devil.

In this way he could cause good or bad things to happen to his friends or enemies. Every European state recognized witchcraft as a crime and executed witches and wizards.

In Massachusetts, some people nailed horseshoes to the doorpost to protect themselves against evil spirits.

If a cross old woman chased the boys she found robbing her apple tree ...

... and if that night one of the boys suffered from a stomachache ...

... it was easy to think the old woman was a witch who had put the "evil eye" on the boy.

In 1692, in Salem Village within the Massachusetts Bay Colony, a witchcraft madness broke out. Reverend Samuel Parris had in his home a West Indian slave, Tituba. To amuse the young girls in the family, Tituba told stories of witchcraft from her former home.

Later, the girls claimed that Tituba had bewitched them.

Beaten by her master, Tituba, to save her own skin, confessed and accused two other women of being her accomplices.

The madness spread like a fire out of control. Fearful people accused others to pay off grudges or to keep from being accused. Accused people were sent to the trial court from towns all over the colony.

Some accused people confessed to broomstick rides, attending witches' sabbaths, and all the other things they had heard that witches were supposed to do.

Those who confessed were imprisoned but not executed. It was those who refused to plead guilty or to accuse other persons who were condemned.

In all, 14 women and five men were taken in carts through the streets to Gallows Hill, and there publicly hanged.

When this shameful episode was over, a new phrase was added to our vocabulary. The phrase was "witch hunt," and it describes a trial in which hysteria and fear take the place of justice.

In 1636, the same year that Harvard College was founded and Roger Williams was banished, a group of settlers left Massachusetts for the wilderness of Connecticut.

It was a hard trip of 14 days through heavy woods, on foot, and carrying all their belongings.

Soon forts and rough houses were built, and the rich meadows along the Connecticut River were planted with corn.

32

The leader of the Pequot Indians warned that if the English were not stopped, they would soon take all the land.

One morning the Pequots crept up on the settlement of Wethersfield.

The Indians attacked as the settlers were working in their fields.

They left nine of the settlers dead and took two captives.

The colony raised a small army. They marched upon the chief Pequot camp.

At first the Indians held them off, and many settlers were wounded.

Then they set fire to the village, and 400 Indians were killed. The Pequot tribe was left almost extinct.

34

Other groups of English Puritans moved northward to settle in New Hampshire and Maine. New Hampshire soon became a separate colony, but Maine remained a part of Massachusetts until 1820.

The best spot on the Atlantic coast for a colony was not settled by the English. In 1609, Henry Hudson, sailing for the Dutch, first explored the fine harbor we know as New York, and the great river now known as the Hudson.

The Native Americans in their canoes brought furs to Hudson's ship, the *Half Moon*, to trade for iron axes, brass kettles, guns, scissors, and other items.

In 1626, Peter Minuit, for the Dutch government, bought Manhattan Island from the Native Americans for trinkets worth less than $100.

Soon windmills and rows of neat brick houses marked the site of New Amsterdam.

The colony of New Netherland stretched up the river to Albany. Dutch settlers were thrifty and hardworking, but the traders who owned the land cared only for profits from trade. They refused to give settlers the land they worked, protect them from unfriendly natives, or let them share in the government.

So the Dutch settlers refused to fight when, in 1604, the English, under the Duke of York, started to take over the rich area.

Headstrong Peter Stuyvesant, director general, called his council together and demanded a brave defense. But the councilmen simply went home and locked their doors, and New Amsterdam became New York.

In Europe, a growing new religious group, the Quakers, were hated by the ruling classes and by other religious groups. The Quakers rejected religious authority, believed that God was present in every man, and that all men were created equal.

When they first reached Boston in 1656, they were thrown into prison.

They were banished from Massachusetts and other colonies. Some were tortured and killed.

36

William Penn was a Quaker. In 1681, King Charles of England gave him a royal grant for a colony in America. This land reached from New York to Maryland.

Penn promised religious freedom, humane government, and cheap land. He also gave fair treatment to Native Americans and payment for their lands. Settlers came from England, Scotland, Ireland, and Germany.

When Penn himself reached the colony to be known as Pennsylvania, both natives and white settlers joined in cheering him.

In 1638, Sweden set up a colony of Swedes and Finns on the present site of Wilmington, Delaware.

They brought log construction and the log cabin to America. It was so well-suited to pioneer housing that it spread all over the frontier.

After the Duke of York took over New Netherland, William Penn persuaded York to give him the land on the Delaware River. This became the colony of Delaware. William Penn and a group of Quakers also bought the Jerseys from York. This became the colony of New Jersey.

In England, in 1632, King Charles I agreed to cut a slice out of northern Virginia for his friend, Lord Baltimore.

The King gave Lord Baltimore a deed for a colony to be known as Maryland.

Lord Baltimore wanted to build a colony for Roman Catholics. They had no legal rights in England. However, he admitted Christians of all beliefs, and the Catholics were soon outnumbered. To protect the Catholic minority, a Toleration Act was passed by the Maryland Assembly.

In Massachusetts, only the Protestant Puritans were allowed. It was a step forward to have Protestants and Catholics living peacefully in the same community.

In St. Mary's, the original Maryland settlement, they even worshipped in the same building.

The system of legal religious freedom that grew up in Maryland, as in Rhode Island and Pennsylvania, became one of the cornerstones of the American republic.

In 1668, Charles II gave rights to land south of Maryland to eight of his courtiers. This land developed independently and was later recognized as the colony of North Carolina and South Carolina. Development there was marked by growing industries and a policy of religious freedom.

At that time some 1,500 pirates were sweeping the seas, looting any vessel they could catch. Driven from their main hideout in the Bahamas by the British fleet, they made their last stand in sheltered coves along the Carolina coast, where they were a danger to settlers.

It's Blackbeard!

One of the most famous was Black-beard. One day, his fleet appeared before Charlestown Harbor.

He captured a ship that carried many leading Charleston citizens.

We're defenseless. What else can I do?

Blackbeard sent a demand to the governor for medicine and other supplies. Otherwise he would send back only the *heads* of the prisoners!

After the supplies were sent, the prisoners arrived home almost naked. The pirates had robbed them of even their clothes.

Of the 13 original states of the Union, Georgia was settled last. In 1732, King George II gave a charter for the southern, unsettled part of the old Carolina territory to General James Oglethorpe.

Poor fellows! We will take them to Georgia and give them each 50 acres of land.

The British government wanted settlers in order to resist the Spanish in Florida. General Oglethorpe wanted to give debtors, held in English prisons, a fresh start in the New World.

It's hard to believe that I am a free man with my own farmland!

There were about 3,000 colonists settled in Georgia. Half of these were English, and the rest Germans, Swiss, and Scots. This colony's founding eventually led England into war with Spain. General Oglethorpe was friendly with the Native Americans, so they supported him against Spanish Florida. But Spain continued to own Florida for another 30 years.

The 13 original colonies were settled mainly by the English. English became the common language. English laws and customs were followed. The English common man had more rights than people from other European countries, and he expected more of the same rights in the colonies.

There were no homes for rent when colonists began to arrive in America.

They dug a hole in the river-bank and roofed it with tree limbs and bark.

Most came bringing almost nothing but a willingness to work hard for a better life for themselves and their children. So it was with William and Elizabeth Hard, Quakers from England, who arrived in William Penn's Philadelphia in its earliest days with little but their cot.

I am so tired and so hungry. Why did I move to America?

When William went off to find stones for a chimney, Elizabeth threw herself on the dirt floor and wept.

42

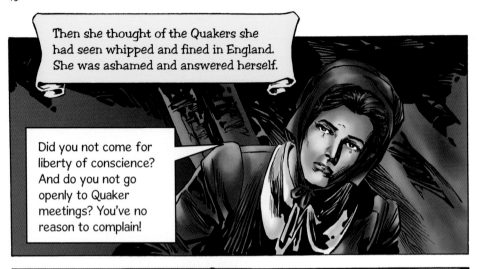

Then she thought of the Quakers she had seen whipped and fined in England. She was ashamed and answered herself.

Did you not come for liberty of conscience? And do you not go openly to Quaker meetings? You've no reason to complain!

Oh, cat! You have brought us a fine dinner.

So the Hards and their cat dined well on rabbit that night. Later they had a more comfortable home and no worries about food. Later still, they had silverware with their family crest on it: a cat with a large rabbit in her mouth.

By 1750, the colonies had grown to 1,500,000 people. A French traveler called the new type of person that developed here the "American." Colonists developed independence and self-reliance. They also learned how to cooperate with others, which was so necessary for survival.

★ ★ ★ ★ ★ ★

In 1750, nine out of ten Americans made their living from the land. But, since geography was varied, different regions developed in different ways.

With long, cold winters, New England was a land of hills, mountains, and rocky soil. The farms were small and not profitable, but a hard-working farmer could make a living and be self-sustaining and independent. He also needed a hardworking wife and children, for all contributed their share.

If you visited a colonial farmer, he might tell you ...

My farm gives me and my whole family a good living.

In the kitchen, his wife makes candles. A daughter spins wool from their sheep to make the clothing they will wear.

The big, crude wooden plow is their most useful tool.

Since it is winter, the men are cutting logs, which the ox team will transport over the snow.

Fishing, lumbering, ship building, and trading also became important businesses. Whaling was perhaps the most exciting and dangerous occupation.

Whale oil was valuable as fuel for lamps. Whale bones and ivory were also in demand. As many as 150 whaling vessels operated out of Nantucket and others from other New England ports.

When a whale was sighted, the lookout gave the cry.

Thar she blows!

At about 10 feet from the whale, the skillful harpooner would thrust his weapon.

The hurt and enraged whale would either try to slam the boats to bits with his tail or tear off with the boat in tow on a "Nantucket sleigh ride."

The middle colonies of New York, Pennsylvania, Delaware, and New Jersey were very good for farming wheat and other cereals for export. There were many small farms worked by the owners. There were also large estates requiring many servants.

The Conestoga wagon was developed for hauling freight. Stronger draft horses were bred from stock brought over by Dutch and Flemish settlers.

Conestoga wagons were usually drawn by four to six of these horses and would become the covered wagon that took many settlers over the Oregon Trail.

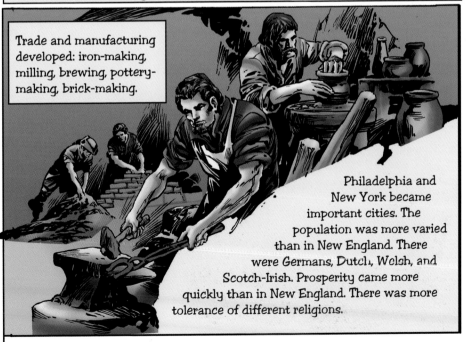

Trade and manufacturing developed: iron-making, milling, brewing, pottery-making, brick-making.

Philadelphia and New York became important cities. The population was more varied than in New England. There were Germans, Dutch, Welsh, and Scotch-Irish. Prosperity came more quickly than in New England. There was more tolerance of different religions.

The southern colonies had small farms but also developed many large plantations of a thousand or more acres. Though many large things would grow well, a few special crops were so profitable that the big growers concentrated on these.

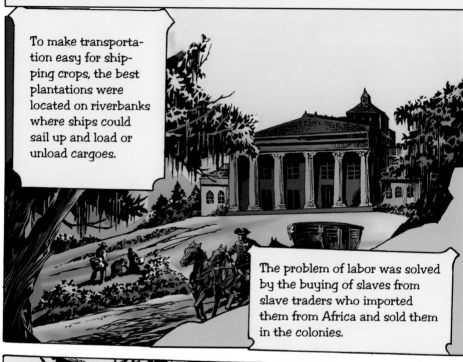

To make transportation easy for shipping crops, the best plantations were located on riverbanks where ships could sail up and load or unload cargoes.

The problem of labor was solved by the buying of slaves from slave traders who imported them from Africa and sold them in the colonies.

Coming by boat, a visitor would first reach the wharf and the tobacco-drying sheds nearby.

As a traveler you would be warmly welcomed both for your own company and because you might bring news from other plantations where you had stopped along the way.

Do you have news of our friends at Westover?

They're just fine. Miss Charlotte was ill, but she quickly recovered.

Near the big house there were smaller buildings: kitchen, spinning and weaving sheds, a washhouse, stables, workshops, and a smokehouse. At a distance would be the slave quarters. And all around would be the all-important crops, in this case, flooded fields of rice.

Charleston, South Carolina, was the leading southern port and trading center. Many of the planters and their families spent the brief winter season there enjoying a merry social life.

Each colony had its own form of government. Early laws were influenced by the church and based on English law.

In Massachusetts, the death penalty could be imposed for murder, for treason, for witchcraft, and for not accepting the beliefs of the church. Nineteen Quakers were hanged on Boston Common because of their religious beliefs.

Boston passed the first speeding law in 1655.

Halt! It is not lawful to gallop!

Idleness, gossiping, not attending church, card playing, and throwing dice were illegal in Massachusetts. Boston also passed laws against letting hogs roam the streets unattended.

Church officials not only made laws, but helped enforce them. The county courts punished by whipping, branding, stocks, pillory, and ducking stools. These punishments were mainly to make the guilty person a target of public ridicule. There wasn't much long-term imprisonment because the community needed its workforce.

In early colonial days, marriage was a practical two-person arrangement. Young women were brought to the colonies as wives for men who could afford to pay the cost of their travel.

Captain Miles Standish, a gruff and bashful soldier of Plymouth colony, asked his young friend John Alden to do his courting for him. When John asked pretty Priscilla Mullins to marry the Captain, she made her wish known, replying, "Why don't you ask me yourself"?

John and Priscilla were married.

It was not unusual to have other people taking part in marriage arrangements. Perhaps two young people were attracted to each other at a husking bee. Like most get-togethers of the time, it was planned around a job of work—in this case, husking corn.

A red ear! I claim a kiss!

This was the prize for a lucky boy who found a red ear of corn!

This boy and girl might decide they wanted to marry: But marriage was serious business. The two fathers would discuss the match. Was the girl a good homemaker? Could the boy support a family? How much money or land would the girl's father give the young couple?

The early settlers did not have time or money for any entertainment. Work meetings, where neighbors got together to do a job, were turned into social events. They brought friends together for visiting and meals as well as work.

On the first good road in the colonies, from Jamestown to the governor's plantation, there was a quarter-mile straightaway. The governor and his friends raced their horses along this stretch on Sunday mornings after church.

52

Many of the settlers came to the New World for religious reasons. Entire Puritan communities came to Massachusetts at the same time. With many members, they could immediately found a strong Puritan church-state and insist that others abide by their beliefs.

The leading Puritan ministers came to New England, men of great learning, intellectual as well as religious leaders. Two of the most famous were Increase Mather and his son, Cotton.

Cotton Mather was so smart he entered Harvard College at age 11.

He graduated when he was 15 years old.

He became minister of Boston's famous North Church when he was only 20.

As the population increased in New England, new ideas took root. A liberal party rose to combat the conservatives led by the Mathers, and the rigid hold of the church-state declined.

In the middle states, with their many different religious groups, religious tolerance came early. In New England it was longer in coming. But in all sections the reality grew that church and state should be separate and the government should have no power over how a person worshipped.

The governments of the colonies were set up in different ways. But the English king remained the head of the government. Each state had an assembly elected by the voters of the colony.

One of the powers of colonial governors was the right to censor newspapers and other printed matter. Printers were put into prison for articles criticizing the royal government. The royal governor of New York used his office for personal profit. He also controlled the only newspaper, the *Gazette*.

Angry citizens persuaded John Peter Zenger, a poor German printer, to start another newspaper. In 1733, Zenger started the *Weekly Journal*, and most New Yorkers read for the first time the shameful doings of the governor.

Governor Cosby had Zenger imprisoned. Two lawyers who offered to defend him were disbarred.

Copies of the *Weekly Journal* were publicly burned.

The greatest lawyer in the colonies at that time was Andrew Hamilton of Philadelphia. Hamilton was old and ill. The journey from Philadelphia to New York was long and hard. But Hamilton felt that the future of a free press in America was at stake, and he made the trip.

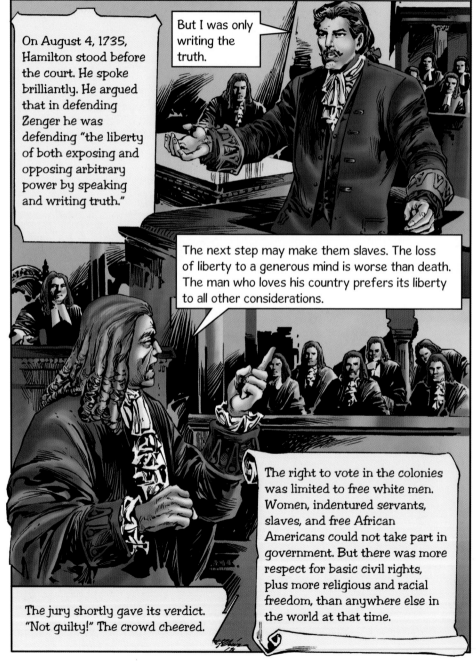

On August 4, 1735, Hamilton stood before the court. He spoke brilliantly. He argued that in defending Zenger he was defending "the liberty of both exposing and opposing arbitrary power by speaking and writing truth."

But I was only writing the truth.

The next step may make them slaves. The loss of liberty to a generous mind is worse than death. The man who loves his country prefers its liberty to all other considerations.

The right to vote in the colonies was limited to free white men. Women, indentured servants, slaves, and free African Americans could not take part in government. But there was more respect for basic civil rights, plus more religious and racial freedom, than anywhere else in the world at that time.

The jury shortly gave its verdict. "Not guilty!" The crowd cheered.